The Zen Life
Spiritual Training for Modern Times

Alex Mill

Zen Life Books

The Zen Life
Spiritual Training for Modern Times

Written, illustrated and designed by Alex Mill

Alex Mill
Zen Life Coaching, LLC
782 Trail Ridge Drive
Louisville, CO 80027

coaching@alexandermilljr.com
http://www.alexandermilljr.com

ISBN-13: 978-1540612953
ISBN-10: 1540612953

Author photograph courtesy of Matt Kosterman Photography

First Edition

The Zen Life

Dear Jennifer,

I hope 2017 brings you nothing but peace, happiness and presence.

In loving kindness,

Alex

For Karen

Contents

A disclaimer... xi

An excuse.. xiii

Thank you... xv

1.   Inside each of us is a critical voice of
     dissatisfaction.. 1
2.   Learning to love learning................................ 9
3.   Patience... 11
4.   Ripping the skin off the snake...................... 13
5.   Love will save you... 15
6.   The Toe-Dipping Dabbler vs. The Deep-
     Diving Master.. 19
7.   Commitments and sabotage.......................... 23
8.   Complete destruction.................................... 27
9.   Karma is comfort... 33
10. Will the real me please stand up?................. 39
11. Unconditional Love vs. Tough Love............. 43
12. The compassion conundrum......................... 49
13. Who you are vs. what you do........................ 53
14. Intelligence or having suffered enough......... 57
15. Our life is shaped by our mind..................... 59

16.	No problem	61
17.	Evoking who you are being	63
18.	My insight story	67
19.	Everything I needed	71
20.	The Mighty Breath Anchor	75
21.	On remembering	79
22.	Laughter, the fast track to here	83
23.	Please take the time	85
24.	Tell them about the dream	87
25.	Peace	89
26.	Slowing down and changing course	91
27.	It begins with me	93
28.	Public Service Announcement	95
29.	Looking for love?	99
30.	Self-care	103
31.	Who has the last word?	105
32.	I do not want this	109
33.	Single best thing to learn in life	111
34.	Friends and clients	115
35.	The beggar and the gift	121
36.	The Mental Muddle (and the trouble with making decisions)	125
37.	The foundation is the first thing to go	129
38.	Results and control	135
39.	*Why are we afraid of getting what we want?*	141
40.	The gift	143
41.	God's dog	145
42.	Another gift	147
43.	Love is not passive	149
44.	Sorrow	153

45.   If apathy and panic aren't the answer, what
        is?..   155
46.   We never know how the story will end.........   157
47.   A lot of love to Chance...................................   161
48.   I wish you well with it...................................   163
49.   *How do I stop caring about what other people*
        think of me?...   165
50.   Keep going..   169

About the author..   171

A disclaimer

"*A dvice is autobiography. I only say what has worked for me, and then others can choose to try it or not.*"

~ *James Altucher*

I am not a Zen master, Zen teacher, guru or anything at all. My own teacher was never ordained as a Zen priest. She does not disclose the identity of her teacher and simply refers to him as "my teacher" or "The Roshi." Yet she expresses a great devotion to him, the teachings and the practice that saved her life. She does whatever she can to share the work with others in the world as a true bodhisattva would. In these ways, I feel like I have adopted her wisdom and the teachings from my experiences of Zen.

This book, like my previous book, *Meditation and Reinventing Yourself,* is filled with stories from my 14 years of training in a Zen monastery as well as my time out in the world as a coach, meditation instructor and public speaker.

These stories have helped me navigate through my own life intuitively and it's my desire to share them here with you.

I see a great need for deep training in peace, compassion, attentiveness, clarity and joy in the world today. This is something many of us have never received in all of our years of learning and living.

I feel extremely blessed that I passed through what I affectionately refer to as "spiritual boot camp" so that I can offer these stories to you now.

I hope they help you.

An excuse

"A priest was in charge of the garden within a famous Zen temple. He had been given the job because he loved the flowers, shrubs, and trees. Next to the temple there was another, smaller temple where there lived a very old Zen master. One day, when the priest was expecting some special guests, he took extra care in tending to the garden. He pulled the weeds, trimmed the shrubs, combed the moss, and spent a long time meticulously raking up and carefully arranging all the dry autumn leaves. As he worked, the old master watched him with interest from across the wall that separated the temples.

When he had finished, the priest stood back to admire his work. "Isn't it beautiful," he called out to the old master. "Yes," replied the old man, "but there is something missing. Help me over this wall and I'll put it right for you."

After hesitating, the priest lifted the old fellow over and set him down. Slowly, the master walked to the tree near the center of the garden, grabbed it by the trunk, and shook it.

Leaves showered down all over the garden. "There," said the old man, "you can put me back now."

The chapters in this book meander and repeat their themes like leaves drifting off branches. Sometimes elements fall out of place. There's no perfect order.

I've noticed that life is a lot like this too.

One of my favorite books of all time is *Zen Flesh, Zen Bones*. The section "101 Zen Stories" captures beautifully the essence of Zen in the lessons expressed in those tales.

As I was arranging *The Zen Life*, I aspired to accomplish the same.

Thank you

ne regret I have about my previous book is that I never included an acknowledgements section.

I was focused on self-publishing it at record speed — in time to have 75 copies printed, delivered and sitting under every seat at Steve Chandler's event, *Reinventing Yourself Weekend*, in April 2015.

I felt that spending time writing and perfecting an acknowledgements section was something that would have prevented me from making that deadline.

At least that's what I heard in my head. Maybe the voices were right. Or perhaps wrong. To me, it's fascinating that the opportunity to express gratitude and credit was the piece that didn't make the cut.

Disirregardless, there's a lesson in this and I know it's significant. Expressing gratitude and credit needs to be more of a priority for me. The lack of it shows up in my relationships with people. I am conscious that showing and expressing gratitude is part of my ongoing spiritual work.

I also know that a moment of awareness and acknowledgement can right lifetimes of wrongs. Here is my attempt to right at least a few:

Thank you to my beautiful, loving, brilliant and compassionate partner Karen Davis. She has been my beacon of light, my champion, and my true love. I cannot even begin to express the thanks and love I have for her. My last book and this book would not have been what it is if it had not been for her.

Thank you and Deep Gasshō to my teacher, the monastery, the monks, the Buddha, the teachings, teachers and sentient beings for the best life training and education I could ever have received.

Thank you to my personal coaches and mentors: Jacob Sokol, who started me on this mad journey of impact and income; Steve Chandler, who deepened my dedication to service as the path to prosperity; John Hruby, who helped me find my way as a man after being a monk for so long; and Melissa Ford, who stands in my desire to lead with love and *be* a professional coach serving my clients instead of pleasing them.

Thank you to Natalie Vargas-Suppi, my yoga teacher in Vineland, New Jersey, for helping me integrate into the world after I left the monastery. Her studio, Peace Love Yoga, became my second home. It's where I soon began offering my meditation workshops monthly to her community and spreading the power of meditation to everyone I could reach.

Thank you to everyone who has ever attended a workshop with me whether that was my *Meditation Workshop*, *The Art of Inner Leadership* with Karen Davis, or *Reinventing Yourself Weekend* with Karen Davis and Steve Chandler.

Thank you to Live Your Legend and Scott Dinsmore for his blog challenge. Because of my participation in his community, I found my earliest fans that stuck with me and helped me create my first offerings to the world: Eric Young and Erin Waterman. Eric made sure that I published my first book, *Practicing Presence*. I didn't realize it at the time, but he was coaching me to success by believing in me. Erin participated in everything I created — she registered for my online retreat, edited my books and became one of my first coaching clients.

Thank you to my brother, Andy. I think he was truly my first real fan and supporter. Whenever I needed help designing my website, Kindnessville, he was there with HTML-a-blazing to get everything exactly the way I wanted it. He is also the one who still, to this day, opens my newsletters first and shows a real interest in what I'm up to.

Thank you to John Shearer, "The Mindfulness Coach," who helped spread the word about my online retreat, *Heart-to-Heart: Compassionate Self-Mentoring*. He put in several "plugs" for it through his Facebook page and gave me the boost I needed in my early days.

Thank you to all the grads that completed my 30-day online retreat, *Heart-to-Heart: Compassionate Self-Mentoring*, and the members of my *The Zen Life* Facebook group.

Thank you to all my coaching clients. I am honored that you chose me to assist you in your journey. You inspire me with your insights, challenges and triumphs everyday.

Thank you to the many coaches I've met, coached and been coached by.

Thank you to anyone I did not mention, which is likely in the several billions at this point.

And definitely last, but nowhere near least, many endless thank yous go to my Mom and Dad. Talk about selfless service. I don't think I will ever come close to living and breathing the unconditional love they have shown for me over the years. I love you so much!

In lovingkindness,

Alex

Inside each of us is a critical voice of dissatisfaction

If you've ever wanted to start something new, change a habit, learn a skill, be more successful, move through life easefully and express yourself authentically — you're probably aware of how challenging that can be sometimes.

Because, let's face it, for whatever reason it's easier to:

- Be distracted by social media
- Eat foods that are less than healthy
- Skip exercise more than we should
- Drop helpful practices like meditation
- Miss time with the important things (and people) we care about
- And spend that time feeling bad about the past and worrying about the future

We do this instead of really taking care of ourselves and being powerful in our personal and professional lives.

Why is that?

Well, in my 14-years of training at a Zen monastery, I studied this a great deal. What I noticed was that under my immediate awareness was a constant stream of thoughts going. We called them "voices." You may have noticed them too. Voices that say things like, "You're too busy to do that course you would love to do." Or, "There's not enough money for you to afford that." Or, "You'll get to it later... tomorrow... or you'll do it next time," and then never do it.

Have you heard voices like these? If so, jot some of them down below. Get them out into the open:

_____

_____

_____

_____

_____

Please note: There's nothing wrong with you for hearing voices. It's *normal*!

Everyone has voices running in their heads. And if you know someone who says that they don't, they may just not be aware of them.

Here's the deal...

These voices are what you need to address before you will ever be deeply free or happy.

That's a pretty bold statement, I know. But listen…

These voices create anything from mild dissatisfaction, to worry, to fear, to overwhelm, to distraction, to stress, to confusion, to feeling bad, to depression, to anxiety, to (you get the picture!)

And there's a great deal of momentum they've generated over a lifetime. Which is why it's so hard to go up against them.

Some people attempt to overcome them in a variety of different ways. Like through drugs. Or they may decide to change careers and do something less taxing. Or ditch certain "toxic" friends. Or try a course on mindfulness. Perhaps even take up yoga or meditation. I know people who have weekly massages and spa treatments just to "get away."

Perhaps you've tried some of these things too.

But if you're like anyone else I've ever known, you may have noticed that even though it helped short-term, it didn't really stick. The book inspired, but then that inspiration faded. Or you had amazingly peaceful experience at a retreat only to find that all your problems and stressful issues were waiting for you when you got home.

It's like the entire experience got erased. Like it never happened and you're back to square one.

This can be so frustrating!

I know. I've had this happen to me many times.

And then when push came to shove, like in a highly charged moment at work, driving on the road or with a loved one — all my knowledge and good intentions disappeared and I *totally lost it*. I flew off the handle.

Then what did the voices say? "Look at you! You know better! You claim to be so 'together', yet you're no better than *they* are..."

And then I got to feel bad.

I'm not saying that the methods I mentioned earlier are ineffective. I meditate and do yoga. What I will say, however, is that they're not going to address the real underlying issue.

And the real issue is...?

The real issue is that the change needs to happen *from the inside* — not by changing the outside circumstances, which is what most people try to do as an attempt to escape or numb out.

Do you know these two quotes by Albert Einstein?

"We cannot solve our problems with the same thinking we used when we created them."

"Insanity: doing the same thing over and over again and expecting different results."

These quotes point to what I did before my Zen training. I spent years listening to and believing an inner self-sabotage system of limited thinking, distraction and feeling like I wasn't enough.

As far as I can tell, everyone everywhere has it and we pass it along through the generations like some negative gene.

"So what's the answer? What do we do?"

Here's my best answer:

Learn a practice that will begin to turn the system in the other direction. It's what transformed my life and the lives of those who came to practice at the monastery.

This practice, and my stories about it, are what I'll be sharing in the following chapters.

The Practice

Learning to love learning

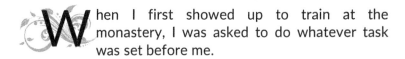**hen** I first showed up to train at the monastery, I was asked to do whatever task was set before me.

I was shown how to do the task. I demonstrated that I learned it. I was corrected if I didn't get it right. I demonstrated it again. If I got it right, then I did it on my own.

This process continued from cleaning outhouses, to chopping carrots, to greeting new guests, to running the kitchen, to operating the small business, to facilitating retreats and workshops.

"I don't know how to" was the *perfect* place to be.

What I eventually learned was that the process of learning itself can be joyful.

And that's exactly what I learned at the monastery first and foremost: A desire to cultivate an attitude of mind that embraced curiosity, wonder, and Zen's beginner's mind. What we called "The Spirit of Inquiry."

Patience

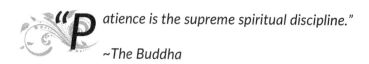 *atience is the supreme spiritual discipline."*

~The Buddha

I don't think the Buddha was talking about the kind of patience in which you don't blow up in anger at a co-worker. I suspect that he was referring to the endurance necessary to practice ending suffering despite all obstacles and resistance. To never swerve from that single-pointed focus.

Many people bring some form of spiritual practice or discipline into their lives. They may create a morning ritual, daily prayer or meditation practice.

At the Zen monastery, we talked about a more powerful way to consider practice: Instead of bringing a practice into our lives, we brought *our lives* into spiritual practice.

In this way, everything that happens to us is lived within the context of practice and nothing is left out.

This made it very clear that the first priority was practice. Practice was the container of our lives and our focus was on how everything else fit in to it.

It became obvious when daily distractions arose to pull us away from our focus by something that seemed more important. Because our lives were a spiritual practice, we were not tempted to lose hope and patience.

Someone who makes this type of commitment becomes very clear that there is no more waffling left.

What that person is saying is, "I'm no longer deciding to practice whenever it feels good or right or when I need it or if I'm in the mood to practice. Practice is my entire life and who I am."

Ripping the skin off the snake

There are two ways:

The violent, painful, cruel and pointless way.

Or the natural, timely and gentle way.

The snake's skin will be shed the moment it needs to be and no sooner.

At the right time.

Only *we* get impatient and rip ourselves apart in our race to success, happiness, and fulfillment.

How can we slow down and move *with* Life and its cues?

To follow the path and see the main view when we arrive at the main view.

Trusting that the main view does not show up earlier but rather when we arrive.

Everything in its due time.

Love will save you

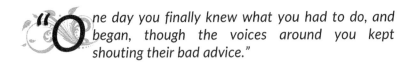

"One day you finally knew what you had to do, and began, though the voices around you kept shouting their bad advice."

~Introduction to Mary Oliver's poem, "The Journey"

When I began my training at the Zen monastery, I made a written commitment to practice for a certain length of time. I committed to a year and then I recommitted yearly for 13 years.

At that time, I shared my intentions and what I would need during my stay (phone calls to my family every Sunday, access to toiletries, dental cleaning appointments, and anything else I could foresee wanting or needing).

I was going in to face "the monster" inside of me. The other monks and my teacher were going to support me on my mission to see how I caused myself to suffer so I could ultimately drop that and end suffering. I was asking them to take ego's escape route away from me by locking me in with it and myself.

Out in the world, I could quit if it got too hard. I knew I could become distracted or something "more important" could come along and I'd go after that instead.

I needed their compassion and support.

I needed to see that "the monster" was in fact a mouse (with a very long and sinister shadow that scared me!)

Fast forward to the beginning of my coaching career outside the monastery:

I noticed that the equivalent to this type of commitment out here in the world was created through the use of money. I saw that the moment my clients invested in themselves, the magic began. The waffling, wavering, weeble-wobbling, half-hearted dabbling disappeared for a moment and the part of themselves who had already succeeded inside of them showed up. These clients metaphorically shut the door on themselves and proclaimed, "Come hell or high water, I'm going to make this happen. I will succeed!"

And you can hear it in their enthusiasm!

The degree of this enthusiasm appeared to be in direct proportion to the size of their investment. The greater the investment, the more on the line and the more value they placed on their dreams and transformation. *The more formidable the door!*

Sometimes this enthusiasm lasted over the course of weeks. However, in my experience, it could vanish before the first payment has been made. A bump into the voices of fear, scarcity, doubt and something wrong could suddenly wake the monster inside and they'd go running into the night for "mommy." Even friends and relatives thought they'd gone crazy for doing this and tried to talk them out of it.

This is why locking the door is so very important.

Because what happens when it is locked is my clients must face everything and avoid nothing. The voices do not want to change. They definitely don't want this type of scrutiny. The voices are very happy with the safe, small, secure and suffering little life they've enslaved my clients into. And I've watched them become identified with these voices. They go pounding at the door begging to be let out. "I made a mistake, I made a mistake... please let's just call this off and give me back my money..."

Compassion does not let them settle for less.

You are adequate to your own experience. In fact, you are more than adequate. You are a hero in this game called Life. If you keep playing, you will face down "the monster." With no escape, insights will drop in and you will shift your focus from a "Really Great Big Hairy Problem" to a gentle, fundamental question, "What's possible?"

Now you are open to solutions! With compassion, you will be supported to face your relationship with yourself and create your dreams. "The negative" has been transformed into "the positive" by just a single shift of focus. The energy of fear will become used by the life force animating you to create a passionate vision instead.

My experience as a coach is that I serve as the door and the compassionate stand I take for my clients. I see who you are and what you are capable of and I will help you realize this for yourself. I will not let you give up on yourself. Because I love you.

The power of love is the most powerful one there is.

I guide my clients into that loving relationship with themselves. I show them that there's life outside the cell. That commitment and willingness is the key.

And love is the pathway through.

The Toe-Dipping Dabbler vs.
The Deep-Diving Master

once asked a coach if she had her own coach and she replied, "I'm in these coaching groups and so I get plenty of support from the coaches in there."

I repeated my question, being more specific, "Do you have a coach that you work with one-on-one? You know, a paid coaching relationship in which that coach works with you on a regular basis?"

She quickly, and almost in an ashamed tone of voice, replied, "No. I don't. I know everyone says I should. But I haven't."

All "shoulds" aside, I shared some of my experiences of having my own coach with her to see if this could help her understand the difference between having a serious, paid coaching relationship versus having a friend, mentor or peer coaching exchange. Here are some of the things I said to her, plus some musings I added to support my recent insights:

The various spiritual practices, weight loss programs, and coaches out in the world are relatively the same (relatively). It doesn't matter what or who you pick. What matters most is that you commit and find your "want to."

If Zen speaks to you and you see your life begin to shift when you practice, then really stick with it and go deep. Meditate and seek a teacher. If a certain diet is the one you would like to try, then stick with it. Find a support group with people doing this diet and keep going. If a coach you worked with resonates with you and you know a difference has been made already (because you have seen results in the session you've had) — make it a point to hire her or him to go as far as you can go.

Lock the door, get the keys away from the voices and throw them away! Stop dabbling! Go the distance!

You see, so many people have a consumer mentality when it comes to practice or commitment. "Let me see what you've got and if you can't give me what I want, then there's another personal development program a click away that promises instant success."

We hop from thing-to-thing-to-thing. Making potholes in our backyards in search of water. Not seeing that what would really work would be to pick a spot, any spot, and *go deep*.

Resistance uses fear to stop us from doing anything that could truly help us. This is why change — even if it's change we say we want — can be so challenging.

Meditate? Eat healthily? Exercise? Do a gratitude journal? Spend more time in nature? Practice kindness and generosity? Learn something new you'd love to learn? Hire a coach to help you fulfill your dreams?

YIKES!

But get distracted? Eat a bag of chips? Sit on the couch? Gripe about problems? Surf the web? Day-dream about what you want to buy? Get lost in habits and putter around endlessly?

VERY EASY!!!

Why?

Because we're being scared to death by anything that could successfully turn us loose from the conditioned voices in our heads.

On autopilot, these voices are in control.

If we were to get present and start calling the shots in our lives, then the jig would be up. *We* would be free to live the *audacious* lives we were put on this planet to live and *they* would be *out of business.*

I like to reassure people by telling them that resistance is normal.

Yes, if you commit to selling all your belongings and move to a Zen monastery (what I did) your belly will become filled with nest-kicked hornets and freak out. Yes, if you invest more money into your coach than you have to your name (what I did) you will not be able to sleep at night because the voices will pound you for being a crazy fool.

But if success, happiness, fulfillment, moving toward freedom, living the life you were meant to live, choosing *you* over the voices and attaining mastery are what you want, then you know that resistance will be part of the journey.

And they're only part of it.

Feeling the discomfort, hearing the voices shrieking, taking the leap and doing it anyway *always* puts the power back into your camp.

You are training yourself to choose freedom as a function of *who you are*. Every time you do that, you are trusting your actions more and your life will start to expand with possibility.

And this is when things start to really get interesting!

Commitments and sabotage

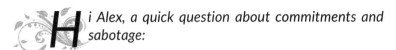i Alex, a quick question about commitments and sabotage:

I managed to work out 10 minutes every day for almost three months. If I didn't do it for a day or two, I would get right back into it.

Now I haven't really worked out in a month. It's that glass ceiling thing again! I keep hearing, "You are so busy, you're doing all these other things, you don't like exercise..." and I convince myself that it doesn't matter so I don't have to beat myself up.

Now that's a total pattern, right? Like with your online retreat.

When I think about, "Just do it now/sneak a day from the voices" the voices say, "It's pointless if you don't do it regularly and you won't do it regularly if you don't really commit. If you *commit, it will be stressful and you will punish yourself for not doing it."*

Any thoughts?

Yes. Make a commitment to something (like working out) and pay attention to see what happens. It doesn't matter what you commit to, whether it be meditating for 5 minutes upon waking, tidying up the house for 20 minutes per day or sending a weekly email to someone that brightens their day.

Whatever it is. Make an agreement with yourself to do it.

Next: Pay attention to how you do — or do not do — what you agreed to do. What do the voices say? Are they enthusiastic and excited? Or are they resistant and complaining? Do they compare your success to others? Or do they distract you from remembering your commitment entirely so that you "forget?"

Or something else?

Pay attention to all of it. Be a super sleuth.

If you get derailed, simply recommit. Don't buy into the voices' assessments of you.

Drop them and jump into the game again.

See how they throw you back into the pot.

Get out.

Back into the pot.

Get out.

See everything you can about *the process*.

Awareness is *key*.

Pay attention. Believe nothing. Don't take anything personally.

Commit *only* to see and learn everything you can about how you do, or not do, *everything*.

Complete destruction

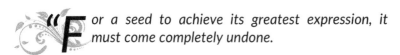*or a seed to achieve its greatest expression, it must come completely undone.*

The shell cracks, its insides come out and everything changes.

To someone who doesn't understand growth, it would look like complete destruction."

~ Cynthia Occelli

Based upon the many conversations I've had with people out in the world, it's become clear that most folks have some romantic fantasy about what it must have been like for me to train in a Zen monastery. After I mention my time there, I notice their eyes become dreamy and I imagine picturesque scenes of monks in robes sitting around under trees all day peacefully meditating.

No obligations. No work. A simple life of chanting, burning incense and bliss.

I can assure you that *nothing* could be further from the truth. We worked our "you-know-whats" off. From early in the morning until late at night — service was our lifestyle.

The retreatants who came from all over the world were our number one priority. That meant cleaning, cooking, tending to their needs, building hermitages for them to reside in, facilitating, and doing our own training amidst all of that work.

Not to mention all the spiritual opportunities that popped up along the way ("spiritual opportunities" is code for "stuff we didn't want to have happen").

Sometimes it felt like all the training I was getting was going to destroy me.

Here I was — here we *all* were — really good monks working so very hard, and then something went amiss and our teacher would swoop in to metaphorically, "shove our noses into it."

"What happened with that!"

This is what I heard when I looked up from the food I was prepping and saw my teacher heading toward me on the first night of our away retreat.

I was the cook, cooking for 45 retreatants, and just a moment ago the head monk came to check in with me about how the meal was coming along. That's when I'd discovered I made an assumption. I thought the evening meal was starting at the "usual time," 6:00 pm. but it became clear that the schedule said it was in fact 5:00 pm.

"Oh boy..." my mind started to reel as the head monk walked away with the bad news.

So now my teacher got involved and I stammered some lame answer back to her, "I, I th-thought it was the same time as always..."

Really. Bad. Answer. Assumptions are like the plague. Assumptions meant I knew I needed to check the schedule (insight) but the crappy voices talked me out of doing what I _knew_ I needed to do (sabotage) and now, here we were, scrambling around trying to make a meal happen at warp speed. As a result everything was going to be late and I would likely face a royal beating from the voices (spiritual opportunity).

The truth is, I had so many of these experiences. It seemed like I needed to burn through this habit _repeatedly_ in order to get to the other side of it.

And no sooner did I have a big "ah-ha" moment that freed me up in one area of my life that I had been struggling with, when another challenge cropped up for me to tackle.

Sigh.

I hated this process. I got depressed. I resisted. I got angry. I cried. I wanted to quit. I was afraid.

It felt like everything was coming undone and I couldn't hold it together any longer.

Which was my problem. I tried so very hard to hold it all together.

You see, the ego wants so desperately to look good, fit in, be approved, be liked and please others.

My teacher would have none of it. What the ego accomplished was a whole lot of suffering for me and a whole lot of dysfunction for all those around me.

From her point of view, I was much better off without it.

What I soon came to realize was that this training and all of the difficult feedback I was getting was really my experience of the ego becoming completely undone and destroyed.

It was being destroyed so that something more wonderful could be freed up to express itself.

And I would never have gone so far for myself, through all of this, by myself. I would have sought comfort or the easy way instead. So don't let anyone fool you that growth doesn't come with this amount of challenge.

In order for something to *become* something else — everything that was there previously needs to completely *fall away*.

This happens in our bodies, in our lives, in others and in Life all around us — *all the time*.

Life is flux.

Many times it looks and feels like *a dying*.

"And the day came when the risk to remain tight in a bud was more painful than the risk it took to blossom."

~ Elizabeth Appell

Why would I think it should be any other way?

Karma is comfort

I n my training, I learned early on that everything I think of as me and who I am is complete and utter fiction. This fiction is Karma.

"Who I am" is held together by beliefs I've collected since I was born. Many are cherished by those within my culture and condemned by those outside of it.

What's true?

Well, that depends on whom you ask. I can't even sort out all of these inconsistencies and identities in my own mind. One moment I'll "seize the day" and in another moment I'll "save for a rainy day."

Identities are a funny thing.

When I showed up to train at the monastery, nobody asked me what I did for a living or what my talents were. I found out that if the monastery knew I was good at something (for example, if I was a chef) I was guaranteed to be sent to do working meditation as far away from my area of expertise as possible (i.e., nowhere near the kitchen. More like hammering a roof together on top of a hermitage!)

Why? Because training wasn't about what was most efficient and nor was it about being the most valuable player. Training was about dropping all of these egocentric dances we do to prop ourselves up and maintain our worldly social masks.

"Hello, my name is Alex and this is what I do. I'm from here, I enjoy this, and I dislike that..."

I learned that my inner stories were the source of my struggles and no one at the monastery was interested in them. My job was to look for a deeper value that wasn't tied to any of those stories by showing up and committing to the One Rule.

And that One Rule was to see how I caused myself to suffer so I could drop that and end suffering. In that, I would be shown my true value.

Sometimes I needed to have things shaken up.

For example, one day I expected to be working in the garden and then suddenly I was pulled out to fold letters and stuff envelopes in the dining hall.

My head would run through all the possible things I could have screwed up that would have caused them to "punish me" by switching things around. "What did this mean?" You see, I wanted to be in the garden.

Not that the other monks or my teacher were plotting my spiritual opportunities. After years of training, being in the work director's shoes and creating the assignments, I realized that no one was thinking about me on a personal level *at all*. We were given tasks and responsibilities because *someone* needed to do them. There was often little or no significance given as to who was going to do what other than, "Who was free right now?"

As a monk progressed in her or his training, after showing up and saying "yes" repeatedly, eventually bigger and bigger things to say "yes" to were presented to that monk.

I went from cleaning the outhouses to chopping carrots; from chopping carrots to heading up the carrot chopping crew; from head of the carrot chopping crew to the cook (who was responsible for the entire kitchen). Then I went on to become the work director (who was responsible for what everyone at the monastery was doing). Then to facilitator, facilitating group discussions. Then I facilitated retreats. Then I created the curriculum for those retreats. After that, I began offering guidance appointments and leading satellite groups all over the country.

It was a big "Yes-Fest." At every turn, I went up against internal resistance and the voices. Here were some of the usual suspects:

"Who on earth are you to do that?

"You have no idea what you're doing.

"You've never used power tools before!

"They're going to find out exactly what kind of loser you are!"

There was nowhere to hide. The experience was an elaborate identity disassembling operation.

Luckily, the support I received along the way was enormous. I was never allowed to go unconscious or just cruise. Ever.

To assist me in staying conscious and on my toes, the schedule was fluid and alive with whatever the moment demanded.

I remember the monks were once woken in the night to tie down an enormous tarp that had been blown off a hermitage we were working on by a storm. On another occasion, I landed from my flight after visiting my family on the East Coast, took a bus to our away retreat facility, walked to the building tugging my carry-on behind me and was informed that I was now the cook for the retreat. All I could do was put on my apron and prepare the upcoming meal for 30 retreatants.

Freeing myself of Karma, required that I roll with all of it. I was on a training ground for spiritual combat — locked in a tumultuous boot camp for my soul and it felt like God and The Devil were wrestling for it!

You see, so much of what is desirable out here in the civilized world is seeking out and claiming whatever creates the greatest amount of ease, comfort and unconsciousness. The status quo. Unfortunately, playing small is a death sentence for the heart.

Nothing grows in a comfort zone.

"I only engage with these types of people.
"I can't do that because I have children.
"I've been in this job for over 20 years. I can't just up and leave.
"I've always been this way and so I'm not going to ever change.
"I don't have the money, so I'll pursue that dream later.
"I'll do that — after I retire."

But "doing what I've always done" was exactly what got me into trouble over-and-over again. I wanted to break free of those limiting habits, beliefs and ways of being. I could not be tied down to that which limited me.

Sometimes it took what I called "kicking the hornet's nest." Or tipping the boat over when I was afraid to rock it. To become an active, compassionate disruptor.

Sometimes we had assistance.

There was a story about a monk who trained at the monastery before I arrived. She was a Catholic nun, Sister Phil. Apparently she never bought any clothing for herself that didn't come from a thrift store. She wouldn't allow herself to. Her identity was tied to being frugal with every aspect of her personal life. One day, her working meditation assignment was to take an envelope of money and go clothes shopping for herself. Her only guideline was that she could only buy retail. Nothing could be used or from a thrift shop.

Freeing her was more important than preserving her identity.

Now please don't read this with the idea that there's anything wrong with used clothing or being frugal. Or, that there's something wrong with doing the same thing repetitively (I meditate and have the same morning rituals every day).

Stick to the spirit of the teaching — to go beyond Karma or comfort — and allow yourself to see where you could turn loose the voices and embrace something much bigger, freer and all encompassing.

The spirit of challenging Karma is one of play and adventure. The mission is to free the human spirit so you can pursue what the voices in your head scream "no" to.

Just to prove that you can.

Will the real me please stand up?

*There's so much noise in my head. How can I figure out the difference between the voices in my head and what's actually useful information? You know, authentic **me**! Intuition.*

Help! Who do I listen to?

I get it. There's some subtle stuff going on here. I spend a bit of time with my clients ferreting out who's who and what's what in their heads so they can get clear and just *go*. So they can be unencumbered and free.

I like to start by showing people how to spot a voice. Once you experience it and *see it*, things just start to click. So a brief exploration here might help sort out some confusion.

A voice speaking to you from "something wrong and not enough" is not your friend. This is not the voice of God, your Higher Self or anything you want to bother entertaining. It lives in The Dark Room. We can keep it there.

To go a little deeper, this voice has a qualitative feel to it that gives it away. Here are some ways I like to describe it:

It's shifty, manipulative, seductive, urgent, bargaining, debating, conniving, whiny, mean, berating, and impatient. It makes excuses and it reasons its way into existence. It loves to be right and it loves attention — *all of it*! The attention of others and your own. In fact, that's how it keeps you out of the present and out of The Light Room.

When you're engaged with it (being unconscious) it works its magical con job on you. What's even subtler is that it will argue with itself — leaving you in the middle — baffled and struggling to figure out what to do or which side to believe.

The voices may even pretend to be your friends. Standing up for you "for your own good." Or talking you into doing something that will "take care of you," like sitting in front of the television with a tub of ice cream after a long, hard day's work instead of meditating like you committed to doing.

But don't fall for it.

The voices expend a great deal of mental energy at *your* expense. Thinking, thinking, thinking. In fact, this is the socially acceptable way the voices camouflage themselves. They claim that they're just you "thinking."

I often share the image of Rodin's *The Thinker* to illustrate the kind of suffering involved when we're entertaining the voices in our heads through "thinking."

Please note that *The Thinker* does not look like a happy camper!

Unconditional Love vs. Tough Love

Here is an exchange I had with Mary, a participant in my online retreat, *Heart-to-Heart: Compassionate Self-Mentoring*. She left the following comment after doing the assignment for Day 24:

Mary

The mentoring practice I did in today's assignment contributed to a kinder voice to myself this morning when I didn't get out the door to exercise quite as early as I planned. It felt good to have a more compassionate coach inside my head that didn't berate me for exercising a bit later.

I also re-listened to the mentor assignment today. I was able to tap into the positive emotions of having a kind, supportive mentor that also has high expectations for me, and I could feel today how good that felt.

However, still wrestling with the idea and amount of "unconditional love" vs. "tough love" that I want my own mentor/coach inside my head to have. Yes, it was nice to have a compassionate mentor today, but tomorrow I want the one who is going to get me out the door early. I am still feeling there is sometimes conflict between compassion and self-discipline.

Alex

Interesting. How is there any conflict between compassion and self-discipline?

What if you and your inner mentor got together to make a plan for you to recommit to your goal of getting up earlier in time for exercising? What if, instead of abuse or soft "love" (basically two sides that don't work), your mentor was there to say, "Okay, Mary, you made your commitment to be out the door at 5:00 am and you are a person of your word. Time to get going and get to the gym. How can I help you succeed?"

That's a very firm, honoring, loving, integrity-filled response.

Compassion is *not* soft "love" with a voice that essentially says, "Oh honey, I know you made a commitment to meditate for 5 minutes after work today... But it was such a crazy day! Sitting in front of the tube with a tub of Ben & Jerry's would take so much better care of you."

Nor is it, "Get the #@!*&% off your derrière and meditate, you loser!"

I would love for you to have these guidelines, practices and commitments help you and your mentor to work together better in a more conscious, compassionate way. For you to get that doing these activities really don't matter as much as *you* do.

I would love for the rest of this retreat to be a deep honoring of Mary — *you* — who tries so very hard and is worthy of your respect, attention, love and guidance.

In lovingkindness,
Alex

"Nothing can stop students with the right mental attitude from achieving their goals; nothing on earth can help students with the wrong mental attitude."

~An adaptation of a quote by Thomas Jefferson

The compassion conundrum

What is compassion? What if we have been using the word compassion to describe "nice and polite" all along? What if compassion had nothing to do with social niceties? What if it wasn't something we could describe by naming actions that were observable from the outside? What if, rather, they were expressions arising from within?

Many leaders are wary of learning mindfulness. The fear is that this relaxed and peaceful state will soften their company's decisive actions. Meditating business professionals will not fire incompetent employees. They will not compete with the ruthlessness required to create success. Or they will miss opportunities because they just won't care.

But compassion, mindfulness and meditation are not about being passive doormats. In fact, it is quite the contrary.

Zen stories are filled with Zen masters wielding staffs, not just to help them walk in their old age, but to knock unsuspecting (and unconscious) Zen students *awake.*

Today, when I'm coaching my clients, I often hear the compassion conundrum arise.

"My husband," one client complained, "He doesn't want to clean the dishes and so I feel the rage build up. Then I catch myself and realize I can just do the dishes myself."

It's often a choice between being a nasty porcupine or an enabling pushover. Somehow these two polarities ping-pong off of each other and *the real* compassionate solution just never finds its way to the surface.

For example, she and her husband could sit down and agree on how to handle those dishes.

Imagine compassion asking, "What is the best for all?"

What if learning or *awakening* was the best for all? What if compassion was not about others having a pleasant experience or others liking me and everything I do?

What if compassion required us to *awaken* and *transform* instead?

What if the most loving and compassionate thing I could do was to help free you from the bondage of your socially conditioned reactions and habits?

What if I took a stand for who *you* were in all your possibility by asking, "What is the most empowering experience you can have? How can I creatively open your mind and assist you? Even better, how can this opening assist you to help yourself?"

There are times when I interfere and it doesn't look like compassion at all. It's fierce. Because in order for you to wake-up to a new way of *being*, sometimes more enthusiastic measures may be needed.

As I learned at the monastery, some students will respond and learn from a whisper. Others, however, will require a "spiritual 2×4" over the head!

It comes from speaking the truth in a way that will be heard by the listener.

Imagine a man gripping two high-voltage cables and being electrocuted. They're killing him and he can't let go. If I grab hold of him, I run the risk of dying along side of him. How can I save him? Well, I can jump in, grab the enormous board next to me and whack him off of those wires as quickly as possible.

From the outside, it appears as though I'm doing him injury. But anyone who understands what is truly going on will see that I am saving his life!

What is most compassionate?

Who you are vs. what you do

Imagine a dot on a whiteboard.

That's who you really are. The dot represents authenticity. Everyone, deep down, wants the same thing. To be okay, to do the best they can, to be accepted, to get attention, to survive and to make some contribution.

I seriously doubt many people wake up in the morning and say to themselves, "I wonder how I can royally screw something up today." Or "I wonder how I can have as many people as possible hate me."

Yet it's surprising how most of us treat others and ourselves from the assumption that these are our motives. That they, and we, are intrinsically bad.

Now, imagine a circle drawn around this dot. This circle represents our conditioned behaviors. These behaviors run the gamut of what human beings are capable of expressing. From the most atrocious acts of cruelty to the most inspiring acts of kindness. They encompass the varying degrees of everything we like and dislike about others and ourselves.

What I have learned is that we confuse people's conditioned behaviors with who they are. We say, "I hate criminals." Or, "I can't stand my husband." Or, "My kids drive me crazy."

I would argue that more accurate statements are, "I hate the crimes that people commit." And, "I can't stand it when my husband leaves his socks in the sink." And, "It annoys me when my children ask me questions all day long."

If we could step back, remove ourselves from the stance of "the other as the enemy," and see their behaviors as the issue, then we have an opportunity to do something about addressing those behaviors *directly*.

This is especially true when I work with couples in relationships. So often I see two people who have their horns locked — wrestling against each other — vying to win "the battle." When I look underneath, I often find that they really do love each other. Sometimes I have them imagine facing each other. Then I ask them to put between them this "Big Hairy Awful Problem" (BHAP). I show them that the only thing between the love they have for one another is this BHAP.

What if instead of both of them fighting each other, they got on the same team and worked *together as a team* to figure this out? What if they sat down and brainstormed all the ways to solve the BHAP together? All of their attention that was previously against each other can now be refocused on the BHAP. What could they do *together* to tackle this BHAP? How could they support each other through this?

At the end of the day, when you look into another person's eyes, you are seeing their humanity. Something we all share in common. The struggles and the victories. The joys and the sorrows. And while certain behaviors are unacceptable, you, as a being are 100% acceptable.

If you wear your muddy galoshes into the meditation hall by mistake, you are not a bad person. Your behavior is unconscious. But that doesn't make you a bad person.

When we can tease out "the behavior" from "the person," now something can be done. The person is not at fault or attacked. The person is okay.

What they're doing is not okay — but those actions can always be addressed.

The point is to never confuse the two:

The person.

And his or her conditioned behaviors.

Intelligence or having suffered enough

What guides people to spiritual practice? What makes someone embrace personal development?

In my experience, there appears to be two reasons:

1) Having suffered enough.
2) Intelligence.

Unfortunately things fall apart first *before* we find ourselves seeking support. It's the reactionary approach. After the voices have sabotaged our best efforts — our health, our careers or our sanity — we wake up to finally take action. Now suddenly we are *pushed* into it.

Many times, it doesn't take some big drama. For example, I was experiencing mild dissatisfaction when it dawned on me to meditate and travel to a monastery to go deeper. In fact, I thought I had everything that should make me happy and yet it didn't.

Later when I was out of the monastery, out in the world working as a coach, I realized that I was not where I wanted to be in my business and I desired to be making a bigger impact. The "pain" of not being successful was my motivation to hire a coach to help me bridge the gap from where I was to where I wanted to be. Because let's face it, I love my life and I want it to get exponentially better and better. As far as I can tell, there will always be incredible, impossible futures on the horizon and I want do my best to create them!

Luckily this brings me to the other reason for doing the work: It's the intelligent thing to do. It's the creative approach.

While intelligence and joy weren't what drove me to the monastery, it is what kept me there all those years. It's what has me seek out mentors, coaches, and spiritual guides today. It just makes the utmost sense to do it this way.

In an interconnected universe, we are never alone and we needn't ever do it alone.

Our life is shaped by our mind

"Our life is shaped by our mind. We become what we think.

Suffering follows an evil thought as the wheels of a cart follow the oxen that draw it.

Our life is shaped by our mind; we become what we think. Joy follows a pure thought like a shadow that never leaves.

'He was angry with me, he attacked me, he defeated me, he robbed me' – those who dwell on such thoughts will never be free from hatred.

'He was angry with me, he attacked me, he defeated me, he robbed me' – those who do not dwell on such thoughts will surely become free from hatred.

For hatred can never put an end to hatred; love alone can. This is an unalterable law."

~ *Opening verses from The Dhammapada, a collection of sayings of the Buddha.*

All of us are plagued by the voices and struggle with our own habits and behaviors that cause us to suffer.

While I do not tolerate people's conditioned actions, I do see those actions as separate from the human beings who struggle with them. I don't confuse the two.

This awareness opens my heart to compassion because I understand this struggle within myself.

Please consider that we are all authentically pure like crystal clear water. The voices that encourage wrongdoing are the floating debris we listen to and believe. They get us into trouble and fill our hearts with suffering and our minds with confusion.

My hope for all of humanity is that we will see through this façade and practice greater consciousness. Above all, my hope is that we can open our hearts to compassion for the challenge it can be to pass through this life being the best human beings we can be.

"For hatred can never put an end to hatred; love alone can. This is an unalterable law."

No problem

"Our mind is like a clear glass of water. If we put salt into the water, it becomes salt water; sugar, it becomes sugar water; shit, it becomes shit water. But originally the water is clear. No thinking, no mind. No mind, no problem."

~ Seung Sahn

Evoking who you are being

There are two parts inside each of you with whom you can be in conversation: The part that experiences limitation, fear, smallness, anger, wrong and separation; or the part that experiences possibility, excitement, vastness, joy, confidence and power.

In fact, these two parts live in the only two places we can put our attention in any given moment. I refer to these places as "The Dark Room" or "The Light Room."

I find that my life devolves when I stay in dark room conversations. These conversations aren't going anywhere. They're the downward spiral of the ego. As a matter of fact, if I as a coach stay within the superficial aspects of a client's life and get tangled up in the details — the petty dramas and the dysfunction — I will have wasted my time and theirs. That's because the ego has no real interest in anything shifting. Often times it just wants to be right, left alone, or in the company of other gripers, whiners and misery-makers (in The Dark Room).

However, through the power of directing a person's attention, I have the ability to speak to the aspects of this person who live in The Light Room. Sometimes this shift can appear to be like a magic trick. I start speaking and the person begins to feel better, more motivated, see new horizons and transform. That's because I have been actively engaging and directing my conversation to the part of them with whom I want to speak: The person who operates in The Light Room. In a sense, I am disidentifying them from the ego, the smaller parts of themselves and the self-hatred, and evoking their authentic being instead. I am having a direct conversation with the power that animates them.

I'll never forget a coaching session I did with a client who started our conversation criticizing the actions of her partner around the holidays. She was not seeing all the assumptions she was making about his possible motivations. She was dead set upon proving to me how he was wrong she was right. If I decided to get involved in this, to show her what I was seeing, I would either end up as "the enemy" (taking his side),"the advisor" (giving my unwanted opinion) or "the idiot" (not understanding her point of view). Instead, I asked her some questions directed to the part of her who wasn't identified with the blame. For instance, I asked her, "Why do you think he did that?" This simple question encouraged her to stand in his shoes and begin to see another perspective. I asked, "What else?" so we could get even more perspectives.

As she answered my questions, she began to see for herself the story she had created based upon her assumptions. Then I asked her, "Do you think he loves you?" at which point she said, "Yes, of course," and then the tears came and some clarity around how she felt for him and her disappointment. We got to the heart of the issue without dealing with the smoke-and-mirrors "problem."

We then focused on her and the creative part of her who could solve this problem. The part of her who was empowered, saw possibilities, operated from creativity, love and joy. This was the part who could create solutions. The part who *needed* to be in charge of *being* her *full time*.

You see, in our work together, I helped her access this part of herself over-and-over again until she felt like she could *be* that more-and-more often. Because this wasn't just a "relationship with her partner" issue, this was a *beingness* issue. A relationship with *her self* issue.

When she learned to master choosing who she was *being*, which room she was occupying — The Dark Room or The Light Room — everything else in her life began to open up in exactly the same manner.

She put the part of her who needed to be in charge of her life in charge of her life. And that made all the difference!

My insight story

I often share this story in my workshops to illustrate the difference between "insight" (The Light Room) versus "conditioned thinking mind" (The Dark Room).

The setting for my story is at the monastery where I trained. It was early morning, and I was walking along the path from my hermitage to the main building. As I passed the clothesline area, I notice a piece of trash by the side of the path.

Instantly, I had the impulse to pick up the trash.

But on the heels of that impulse, I heard in my head, "Nah, don't bother. You didn't leave that there. Let the inattentive monk who dropped it there come back for it and deal with it. Why are you always picking up after others? Besides, you've got to get to the building. You're the breakfast cook. Don't waste your time with this..."

So what did I do? The only "rational thing" I could: I listened to the voices, believed them and just kept walking.

As I rounded the fence to get to the building, my teacher passed me on the path. She immediately noticed the trash, called my attention to it and asked me if I'd seen it there.

This was a real rock-and-a-hard-place moment for me.

If I said no, I was basically confessing to be an inattentive, unconscious, *bad* Zen monk who was lost in his thoughts so much that he was oblivious to his surroundings — including that piece of trash!

If I said yes, then the next logical question from my teacher would be, "Well, why on earth would you not pick it up? Why would you ignore it and keep walking?" In essence, why didn't I take responsibility for it?

Since I took a vow not to tell lies nor practice believing the fantasies of authority — and truthfully, because I had been *nailed* — I told her what happened:

"I was bamboozled by the voices in my head."

So to recap how all of this works:

An *insight* dropped in to pick up the trash. Insights are quick, complete, and perfect. No manipulation, debating or lengthy dissertations.

Insights are the still small voices that remind you to grab your keys if you're on your way to drive your car. They come up with brilliant ideas for your next book while you're in the shower. If you allow them to, insights can generally guide your life perfectly.

Insights show up in a flash and are often short and illuminating.

On the other hand, the voices elbow themselves in and, in my story, they cajoled me out of doing what I knew was right. All sorts of excuses and "good reasons" surfaced. The quality and the structure of conditioned mind is exactly the opposite of insight. In fact, conditioned mind and the voices attempt to override insight at every turn by obscuring the insight and redirecting my attention to discursive thought.

The end result: I get to feel bad for knowing better and not doing better.

Can you see this in your own life? Because this is what the voices do when we make commitments and have insights. The voices:

- Trick us out of keeping commitments or following through on insights
- Sweep in to beat us up when something goes wrong as a result of believing them
- High-five each other and proclaim, "Mission accomplished!" Not only did they bamboozle us out of doing what we knew to do but they then blamed us for the whole thing

Luckily the monastery was a safe place where I had the opportunity to explore how this all worked. This is exactly what our training entailed. My teacher and all the other monks were on my team conspiring to help me *get* it.

It was up to me to see how insights appeared and to see how the voices worked to sabotage me from following those insights.

The ultimate goal was to catch the voices in action and choose something else. The ideal would be to expose them earlier until I could no longer be fooled. Then to live from insights and compassionate self-mentoring *full-time*.

Everything I needed

 "I asked for strength
And God gave me difficulties to make me strong.

I asked for wisdom
And God gave me problems to solve.

I asked for prosperity
And God gave me brawn and brains to work.

I asked for courage
And God gave me dangers to overcome.

I asked for love
And God gave me people to help.

I asked for favors
And God gave me opportunities.

I received nothing I wanted
I received everything I needed."

~ Hazrat Inayat Khan

Dropping it

The Mighty Breath Anchor

kay, it's simple, subtle, and not too terribly glamorous when used in the context of being present.

But it's effective.

I call the breath your "anchor to the present moment." It's portable, reliable and ever at the ready. You don't need a candle, some positive thought to hold in your mind, a mantra, a place to go or a perfect situation. You just need your breath.

In fact, when I mentioned your breath, did you focus on your breath? This is what happens to me whenever somebody suggests that I focus on my breath: My attention goes directly to it.

I never get tired of hearing about it, because I can never have too many reminders to pause and focus my attention on the here/now. It's what I can direct my attention to whenever I need a refuge.

Take a few moments now to be with your own breath. Really notice the air as it enters your nostrils. Note the temperature of the air as it passes on in. Breathe the air into your lungs and into your body. Notice how your body moves to accommodate the breath. Pay attention to the pause at the top of the inhalation. Then notice how your body moves to release the air from your lungs. Pay attention to the temperature of the air as it leaves your nostrils. Perhaps even make note of that slight pause at the bottom of the exhalation.

There's a lot to that single breath.

Now close your eyes and see if you can imagine the breath entering from the top of your head and filling your whole body — even to the tips of your fingers, the tips of your toes, back up to the top of your head and out the bottom of your feet.

Feel the breath really anchor you. Feel it *ground* you.

Remind yourself to check in with your breath again today. You can even focus on your breath while you are doing other activities like driving, hiking, gardening, painting, and moving from room-to-room.

The voices will protest against all of this attentiveness because they like to spend those times developing their intimate relationship with you. Just the two of you. You know — worrying, plotting, rehashing, distracting, obsessing, depressing, and regretting — real "quality time" activities.

But don't buy it. This moment is where it's at. The action is happening *now* and the place for insight to arise is *here*.

Stop now and set alarms for yourself to help remind you to bring your attention back to the breath at least three more times today.

Go on. Risk it!

On remembering

I was in a business meeting with a fellow monk and my teacher in what we called the Work Director's Office. It was a narrow little space off the monastery's main building that could only have comfortably fit three more people. The one thing that saved it from being a simple closet was the enormous window that spanned the entire length of the wall overlooking an expanse of forest.

That afternoon, we were standing and discussing some monastery issues that needed to be addressed. The other monk and I were making our individual cases for what was most important. We quickly went back and forth with our arguments, hoping our teacher would see the wisdom and logic we presented and choose our course of action.

Suddenly she gasped and interrupted both of us by saying, "How breathtaking!"

I remember looking up at the other monk who stood across from me. I was able to catch her incredulous expression that likely mirrored my own.

I didn't say this out loud, but my first thought was, "What?" (As in WTF!) We both immediately turned our attention to our teacher who was standing between us and against the back wall. Her eyes were wide with amazement and that made us both curious to see what she was looking at on the other side of the window.

So we looked.

The view and the light streaming through the trees were indeed breathtaking. We lived on over 380 acres of stunning forest in the foothills. You couldn't take a step around the property anywhere without some natural beauty stopping you in your tracks.

Immediately everything that seemed so important, my view versus "my opponent's" view, dissolved.

In my head, I could hear the voices scream at how irresponsible my teacher was for getting us off topic. "Couldn't she pay attention to what we were discussing 'in the moment?'" I imagined their beady eyes rolling at how she "sabotaged" our debate. "Hasn't she seen views like this before? Why now?"

But I *got it*. I knew she helped us both disidentify from the grip egocentricity had on us. I could tell by the resistant energy arising in me and how the voices protested. She broke through and got us to the other side. To the present.

You see, when the voices have us and our worldview is small and limited, it's really time to drop it.

There's a bigger picture here and it's waiting for us to see it: Life is magnificent and I can choose to exist in the present whenever I want to.

Yes.

I *understand* that.

Now I just need to *remember* that.

Laughter, the fast track to here

A friend recently asked me, "How does humor play into mindfulness?" I told her that laughter was one of the most powerful tools to disidentify us from conditioned mind.

You cannot simultaneously be stuck, depressed, lost in your story, miserable, or suffering while laughing. The reason: It's not possible to have your attention in two places at once. That's why seriousness is such a serious issue for the ego.

Lost in your mind is exactly where it wants you. Trapped between your ears. Caught in a story. Swept up by the drama.

If you were to get present, be in your body, stay in touch with your senses — laugh, sing or dance (Steve Chandler's L.S.D.) — you would shake loose the hold conditioned mind has on you. You would be here accessing insights. And insights are where all possibilities live.

Even science has proven that laughter "lights up" the same part of your brain that insights do.*

So in the spirit of laughter, insights and instant enlightenment, please find something you think is funny and enjoy some presence *now*!

* Humphrey, Elizabeth King: Laughter Leads to Insight: Happy moods facilitate aha! [https://www.scientificamerican.com/article/laughter-leads-to-insight, May 1, 2011]

Please take the time

"Nobody sees a flower really; it is so small. We haven't time, and to see takes time - like to have a friend takes time."

~ Georgia O'Keeffe

If you hear yourself say that you don't have time for what you know will *really* take good care of you — like meditation, like being healthy, like practicing kindness — then please *stop*...

...and take care of yourself.

Please take the time.

Don't miss the "small" things *here* for an imaginary future *out there*.

The voices would like to speed you along straight to your death.

But refuse to follow along. They are not your friends.

Take the time.

Create the time.

Tell them about the dream

"There was a story on the radio that I love about Martin Luther King Jr. before his famous 'I Have a Dream' speech. The night before his speech, King got a call from President Kennedy asking him not to make the speech. He decided he would make it anyway, but was feeling nothing but doom and gloom and that the race situation in America was his worst nightmare. On the day of the speech, he asked a gospel singer who traveled with him to sing a song that reflected his dark mood. After she sang, he began to speak about the 'nightmare,' and he started losing the audience. The gospel singer who was sitting behind him passionately yelled out, 'Martin, tell them about the dream. Tell them about the dream.' This was enough to get Martin Luther King to pull himself together, and the rest is history."

~ Robert Hargrove

Peace

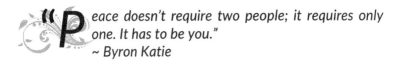 *eace doesn't require two people; it requires only one. It has to be you."*
~ Byron Katie

So often it's a question of, "Who will put the gun down first?"

The metaphorical gun. The get off your separation mind-set gun. The I'm right and you're wrong gun. The I'll do it if you do it first gun.

Today, just drop it all for a moment. Find a situation to simply listen. Listen and then, if you need to speak, reflect back what the person said. Use her or his own words. Watch the need to interpret or put a spin on it, and then drop that. Just listen and reflect.

Don't interrupt.

Find an opportunity to amaze and astonish someone with unexpected kindness and attentiveness.

I know that sometimes I do just enough to get by. It's "too much effort" to thank someone for something I take for granted all the time.

Today, make someone happy and find peace yourself.

Slowing down and changing course

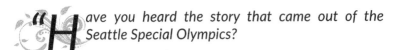

"Have you heard the story that came out of the Seattle Special Olympics?

For the 100-yard-dash there were nine contestants, all of them so-called physically or mentally disabled. All nine of them assembled at the starting line and at the sound of the gun, they took off. But one little boy didn't get very far. He stumbled and fell and hurt his knee and began to cry.

The other eight children heard the boy crying. They slowed down, turned around and ran back to him – every one of them ran back to him. One little girl with Down syndrome bent down and kissed the boy and said, 'This will make it better.'

The little boy got up, and he and the rest of the runners linked their arms together and joyfully walked to the finish line. They all finished the race at the same time. And when they did, everyone in the stadium stood up and clapped and whistled and cheered for a long, long time. People who were there are still telling the story with obvious delight.

And you know why?

Because deep down we know that what matters in this life is more than winning for ourselves. What really matters is helping others win, too, even if it means slowing down and changing our course now and then."

~ Fred Rogers

It begins with me

 "To enjoy the world without judgment is what a realized life is like."
~ Joko Beck

Enjoy.

What a powerful word. As I write this, I'm sitting outside on the porch with a cold — sniffling, sneezing, stuffy, achy-head, fever, (in need of Nyquil™ so I can rest!) — writing and keeping our 13 year old dog, Chance, company. He's not feeling so well either. His back legs have been unsteady and giving out. That, and he has started having trouble breathing while lying down. Poor boy was pacing around for a couple nights. Based upon how quiet and peaceful he is now, I think he's finally started to breathe easier. Did I mention that my partner, Karen, and her son aren't feeling well either? All around is illness, soreness, and pain.

So what's to "enjoy?"

Maybe you're not feeling well either. Maybe what we have is a "walk in the park" compared to what you're experiencing. I know it can be worse.

And yet, there's something to be said for sensations that remind me I'm alive. I've learned this from my mother who is a hero to me in this respect.

So I'm resisting the temptation to call this "bad" or "wrong." I've done what I can to care for others and myself. If I can't do anything beyond that, I've chosen to accept it. Reassurance and consolation go so much further than hatred and condemnation.

"I'm sorry you're not feeling well. I'll do what I can to care for you. I'm here if you need me. I love you."

What I do know is that judgment never made anything better. For the physical pain or the internal suffering.

I'm so glad that peace really does begin with me and we are here to enjoy this precious life.

Public Service Announcement

**S**TOP.

Stress, overwhelm, distraction, feeling bad, self-hate, depression, anxiety, fear, procrastination, self-doubt, disappointment, suffering, anger, misery, mild dissatisfaction, and worry...

Exist in a story

Made up of language

Passing through your head

Disguised as "you thinking"

So you believe it has something to do with you.

But it doesn't.

It's complete and utter B.S.

Designed to do nothing but distract you from...

Possibility, amazement, spontaneity, well-being, creativity, joy, freedom, ease, peace, play, curiosity, wonder, excitement, adventure, confidence and contentment.

PLEASE DO NOT RETURN TO YOUR REGULARLY SCHEDULED PROGRAMMING.

Self-Mentoring

Looking for love?

**A**ttention and approval.

This is what people crave most in their lives. More than comfort. More than survival. More than peace.

Consider for a moment everything you do in your day-to-day life. Why are you doing any of it? If you say your priority is money, go a little deeper. Ask yourself, "What will I have when I get that?"

Here are some more clues: Consider how children are socialized. Why do they end up doing what they do? Pay attention to what their possible motives might be.

Some do everything they can to please or impress the adults in their lives: They get good grades, become the best on the soccer field, or garner popularity. Others, knowing that their siblings are already impressing the adults, may choose an opposite tactic: To get attention from *dis-*

pleasing the adults. They do drugs, get awful grades, attract bad friends, or smash up vehicles.

You see this with gangs and social groups. It's a place where people fit in and get attention and approval.

I was coaching a mother whose son turned to making drugs and using them because he found himself among a group of people who appreciated his creativity and valued what he did. They became his "friends."

He got the attention and approval he sought from them instead of his family.

The sad part is that most of us are still in this child-like relationship with others.

Seeking this approval from outside of us. Demanding it from others. Believing in its lack.

It's all extremely conditional and it's not particularly helpful to us.

"Looking for love in all the wrong places." Isn't that how it goes? Maybe it's there in *that* person? Maybe it's in *that* job? Or maybe it's over there in *that* neighborhood? Or after I buy *that* new car? Perhaps upon retirement, after *that* job is behind me?

Fulfillment is nowhere. And because of this, we do some really crazy things.

"All men's miseries derive from not being able to sit in a quiet room alone."

~ Blaise Pascal

The reason we cannot sit quietly alone is because we have no idea what to do with ourselves. It's boring. We get fidgety. If we sit too long without making a peep or talking to someone, we have to deal with the endless chatter in our heads. We think we'll go nuts. The ego has nothing to reflect itself. Better to drown out the voices with television, relationship drama, alcohol, shopping, gossip...

SOME DAMN THING.

Anything but see who we really are.

Noise, noise everywhere. We can't go too far without music being piped in or televisions blaring or devices zombifying us.

"Men go abroad to wonder at the heights of mountains, at the huge waves of the sea, at the long courses of the rivers, at the vast compass of the ocean, at the circular motions of the stars, and they pass by themselves without wondering."

~ Saint Augustine

The myth is: Happiness, love, attention and approval is all *out there somewhere.* I just needed to find it.

It took me sitting with myself to discover that my Hero's Journey was in search of what was already inside of me.

Under my nose.

The realization that the attention and approval I sought was my very own.

Self-care

Just consider all the goodness that comes from you as you move throughout the world. All the people who rely on you. Everyone who loves you. The world that's different because you're here.

In this moment, acknowledge the work you do. The smiles you create. The laughter you inspire. The contribution you make. The joy you bring.

As you remember all of this, please also remember to show some compassion to this person, *you*, who moves throughout the world with such goodness.

Please be sure to care for the goose that lays the golden eggs.

Who has the last word?

For every action you take, there's some kind of feedback you get.

Cook beans. They turn out well.
Feedback: "Good cook."

Cook beans. Burn.
Feedback: "Bad cook."

What matters most is who has the last word.

Whose ultimate feedback will you listen to? On which side of the fence will you land?

On the side that brings you down, makes you feel bad, calls you an idiot and ruins your day?

Or the side that encourages you to try again, keep going, learn more and move on to the next adventure?

Understanding who has the last word is a powerful distinction to cultivate.

One side hates you.

The other side loves you.

How about you?

Who has the last word?

Imagine

if we obsessed

about all the things

we loved about

ourselves.

I do not want this

I was inspired by a post I'd read on social media in which the author discovered that a friend of his was recently diagnosed with cancer. His friend has children and now they will not experience what it's like to have a mother growing up. He expressed more losses, his own and others.

There is loss and disappointment on all fronts. With a heavy heart, there are often expectations from others and ourselves to look to the positive.

And I say, "All in good time."

First, if you are experiencing difficult emotions, I would suggest that you really be gentle with the part of yourself who is going through this.

Yes, we can always look to find the lesson in every challenge. Or know that we don't have the biggest picture possible.

And we can still have compassion for the tears and the heartache and the disappointment just the same.

If you are experiencing difficult emotions, how can you reassure yourself in this moment?

What would that disappointed, frightened or confused part of yourself want to hear from a loving, compassionate person who cares for her or him unconditionally?

See if you can offer that to yourself in this moment.

Single best thing to learn in life

kay, to me there are actually two things:

One is directing your attention. If you could learn and master only one thing in this lifetime — I would wish for it to be the practice of directing your attention. Because where your attention goes, so goes your life.

The second thing is cultivating a relationship with your self. Once you learn how to direct your attention, you will want to keep it focused on mentoring yourself through whatever circumstances arise.

Together, they are the one-two punch for living an extraordinary life.

Practicing

Friends and clients

During my Zen training, I learned a very useful and powerful distinction that assists me in my personal and professional life today. My own coach knows that I'm still attempting to master it in my business. It's what I call "Being the Friend" vs. "Being the Coach."

You see, inside each of us, there are many subpersonalities and aspects of the self operating under the hood.

For example, you are a different part of yourself when you're speaking to a baby than you are when you're speaking to your mother. And the part of you speaking to your mother is different than the part of you that is speaking to your customers. At least I hope so...

You'll likely see this distinction more clearly in others than yourself.

Take the following scenario: You're having a conversation with a friend and you're enjoying yourself. Then suddenly, your friend's entire personality changes in an instant. One minute he's laughing with you and then the next he's solemn and distant.

That's what we referred to in the monastery as identification, or switching from one aspect of your personality (disidentifying) and becoming identified with another.

We get tripped up and stumble over ourselves when we bring in "the wrong person for the job."

Said a different way, we become unconscious and our survival system takes over. So whichever part of ourselves happens to be around and has successfully helped us through this type of situation before in the past assumes control. Instantly, we become identified with that aspect.

And sometimes this can cause real troubles.

For example, picture a CEO who doesn't get what he wants and suddenly breaks down to become "The Screaming 2-Year Old."

Or imagine a couple on a date. One of them becomes identified with "The Perfectionist" instead of "The Romantic" and then nit-picks everything wrong with the restaurant, the waiter and the date!

Now consider when I am operating from presence and when I'm paying attention. In this state, I have the consciousness to willingly choose which aspect of my personality is the most appropriate for the moment I am in. Disidentified from all of them, I can choose this conscious compassionate awareness to view the situation and be my guide.

I know that when I'm in conversations with my clients as their coach, the most appropriate part for me to play is "The Coach." When I'm at a social gathering, I am "The Connector." When I'm with my dog, I'm "The Snugglewoofer."

My teacher modeled this incredible skill to us consistently. She would be "The Guide" in front of a room full of people, especially at public talks, where she would be speaking profound words of wisdom, facilitating others through their challenges, and transforming lives. Then afterwards she would instantly assume the role of a friendly, casual, and appropriate social personality. It was remarkable how no one would even consider bringing up spiritual questions to her outside of her talks because "The Guide" had left.

Then, just as remarkable, in guidance appointments she would become "The Guide" again.

I remember a time when she offered me a guidance appointment at an airport food court after we had finished an away retreat. During the retreat, I missed my opportunity to have an appointment with her and she generously offered this reschedule on our way back. We were flying home on separate flights and we had some time before our departures.

After she helped clean a table off for a woman wandering around looking for a seat, we began our appointment. At which point, she performed her "magic trick." She went from laughing and reminiscing about how awesome the away retreat we had just finished was to *boom*, "The Guide" was there — offering me powerful guidance. And then just as powerfully, we ended and parted ways to our flights. It was a clean experience from beginning to end.

Today, I find it helpful to understand that both aspects, "The Friend" and "The Coach," live inside of me too. The part that wishes my client, "Good morning. How are you? Wonderful weather," and then moves on to embody "The Coach." All under the supervision of the conscious presence required to determine who and what is appropriate in the moment.

In this way, it is possible to have friendships *and* clients.

But as anyone who has traversed this path before knows, there is tremendous responsibility on the professional to *never confuse the two*. We need to feel the shift within us. We mustn't let the entangling ego and its never-ending desires for social approval, power and personal gains get into the mix. Otherwise we get into some "messy" territory.

So how to go about this?

Many people talk about creating "borders" or "boundaries." This assumes a separate reality that cuts out or puts up walls between others and us. The assumption is that we need to somehow shut our hearts off or hold people at bay.

I would suggest that a more natural and appropriate attitude of mind is to *allow to arise who you need to be* in each and every given moment *within yourself. Call* that aspect up.

For example, *embody* "The Coach" if you are a coach — with presence like an actor would bring to the stage. You *author* this authentic self from conscious compassionate awareness instead of allowing some wandering impulse to take over.

Most people confuse a haphazard, feely, habit driven way as a means to being "authentic."

But don't be fooled. Conscious creation is where the power lies and that's what we have the ability to choose.

It's how really masterful coaches help their clients. They ask their clients to call forth from within themselves the part or parts who are required to achieve their dreams.

It is only fitting that we model this understanding with ourselves, in our own lives and practices, so that we may keep our personal and professional lives in integrity.

The beggar and the gift

A client of mine was struggling in his business. He couldn't figure out how to attract customers who would then see the value of his work so he could ultimately provide service to them.

"I feel like I'm chasing after them and they don't want to get caught." He believed that he needed to get something from others, even though he insisted that he had valuable solutions *for them*.

I asked him if he thought his prospects benefitted from what he offered them. He said that they did indeed. And then I asked him to share some stories and examples of how he had helped them.

He lit up as he went on to tell me about his successes.

It was fascinating that he saw the value he brought; yet somehow when it came to broaching the topic of continuing their good work together, he became a beggar.

I asked him if he could see that the energy he was putting forth was urgently pleading, "Please, please, *please* talk to me so we can do business together! Buy this from me! I *need* your money!"

He saw in that instant that although he never said a single word like that, he didn't have to because the vibe he emitted did all the talking for him. Like the Peanuts character Pig-Pen, who had a cloud of dirt all around him, he had a cloud of neediness surrounding him that drove everyone away.

I asked him, ""What if *you* were the one with the treasure?"

He didn't understand. I could tell by his silence and the look on his face.

"What if you actually walked around and spoke like you had the treasure inside of you. The one your prospects have been waiting for all along to help them with their problems?"

He asked, "You mean, as though I was the one with the answers?" Smiling, "The one who was bearing the gift?"

"Yes, exactly!"

His homework assignment was to test this theory.

With a declaration of his gifts, talents and strengths, he was going to practice *being* The Gift.

He was going to emit golden light out into the world from the glowing treasure house of his heart. He was to see everyone he passed in the streets as a beneficiary of his light and understand that *they* were the ones who desperately needed *him* — not the other way around.

The Mental Muddle (and the trouble with making decisions)

nlightenment is not something you achieve. It is the absence of something. All your life you have been going forward after something, pursuing some goal. Enlightenment is dropping all that. But to talk about it is of little use. The practice has to be done by each individual. There is no substitute. We can read about it until we are a thousand years old and it won't do a thing for us. We all have to practice, and we have to practice with all of our might for the rest of our lives."

~ Joko Beck

So much of our heads are filled with so many options that it can sometimes seem like making decisions is impossible. There are too many choices available. Picking one is daunting — or may even feel paralyzing.

"What if I pick the wrong one? Or what if the other one is better?"

Or, "I've done that before and it was horrible — what if that happens again?"

"What if?" The eternal refrain.

I like to tell people who are caught in a duality battle that, often times, it doesn't really matter what you actually pick. What's important is valuing your own relationship with yourself throughout the decision-making process.

Stay or go? Buy or sell? Love or leave? Cat or dog? Who cares, really? Especially if you are suffering on the path toward making a decision.

You see, the starting place most of us begin is from a place of lack. We believe that we need certain experiences, things, or people in order to feel complete or good. We rarely start with, "I'm okay no matter what I choose."

But that's where I encourage you to begin. Your starting place *is perfect*. (It's perfect because that's where you are. There is no alternative reality in which you aren't where you are in this moment.)

So now that you understand where you are, which is perfect, where do you want to go and what do you want to do?

The rule of the game at this point is that no matter what you pick — flip a coin to make your decision if you must (again who cares?) — you will not entertain any voices that attempt to fuddle you back up.

If it's heads, then you go. If it's tails, then you don't.

Whether it's heads *or* tails, you actively listen to what the voices say. Make lists of their shrieking comments. Get their language out onto paper. Take perfect dictation. But do not, I repeat, *do not*, believe *any* of it.

Theirs are the stories, beliefs, future projections, fears, sabotage systems, and karmic patterns that play out and define the box you live in. Most of them developed in the process of growing up, from something that happened in the past that we survived.

For example, perhaps our hearts were broken in a relationship and so we "decided" that we would never trust anyone or ever fall in love again. Unfortunately, this belief tightened our box down even smaller. Because it is a lie. We don't need to be protected from a fiction. We have no idea how the future will play out.

The voices are like the third wheel in a relationship. There's "stay" and "go" and then there are the voices backseat driving and getting us all in a whirl. With their "yeah, buts…" and "oh no, not thats…"

So pick something you need to decide. Say you choose "to stay."

Notice how the voices start in about how you should have gone and how you are missing out. Or say you decide to go and then the voices start in about how stressful your experience will be and how staying was really the best option.

With the voices, it's a lose-lose situation and an unnecessary mental muddle of suffering.

If you *must* have a third player, who you *really* want to have present to help you is the Inner Compassionate Mentor. The Mentor knows you are okay no matter what you pick. Your starting place is okay. Your finishing place is okay. And all the places in between are okay.

From okay, you pick and choose where you want to go, whom you choose to be with and what you will do when you get there.

It's a game. And if you want to have even more fun — pick the option you don't typically pick. If you typically choose "go", then choose "stay" this time — just to see what the voices will say. Watch how they argue and debate. And then simply practice hearing them without believing them.

This makes *you* stronger and *them* weaker. Eventually, over time, decision-making will become a spontaneous, expressive, and joy-filled process instead of a stagnant, self-conscious, self-doubting and agonizing one that leads to nowhere good.

Happy picking!

The foundation is the first thing to go

I was coaching an entrepreneur a couple years ago who owned his own editing company. His business was such that there were extremely busy periods of time followed by very little business at all.

When I began working with him, he was in the upswing and the season was bringing him a great deal of business. With that, he was feeling the stress of it all.

In our conversation it became clear that he was busy putting out fires, staying up late and allowing the circumstances to dominate his attention so much that it was greatly impacting the quality of his life.

When he contacted me, he told me he was attracted to what I could bring to him because of my background in Zen.

He told me that he himself once had a meditation practice. And that's what piqued my curiosity. The words "once had."

I asked him about it and he confessed that when things got busy, he stopped meditating. In fact, there were two other activities that disappeared from his life as well: Going for walks and writing.

He loved his writing practice very much, so I could tell that being swamped was creating a rather dark period of time for him.

I asked him if he didn't find it ironic that the very things that nourished him and kept him joyful, present and alive were the first things to go. He marveled at that too and assumed it just had to be that way.

"I can't see how to get to those things and still get my work done," he sighed.

Together, in our coaching, we discovered a couple very practical solutions for him that he found powerfully effective over the course of the next few weeks.

He tested them out and then showed up to our sessions excited about how his work-life balance returned.

The first thing I pointed out to him was how conditioned mind (the voices) like to make everything into an "all or nothing" contract. You either meditate for 30 minutes everyday or you don't do it at all.

"Interesting," he laughed.

I joked around with him a little more, "I wonder who comes up with these rules! Perhaps it's the voices? (Twirling their imaginary mustaches...)"

I told him that we hear garbage like this arise between our ears all the time and we just wag our heads and assume it must be true.

So we agreed to five minutes. Then we applied the same principle to the walking and the writing. He didn't have to go for a long hike. Just a stroll around a couple blocks was enough to revitalize him. When we tackled his writing practice, the thought of doing it again lit him up.

What thrilled him the most was his writing topic. He was going to use his creative time to report in on how he was experiencing resistance around meditation, walking and writing! It was going to be his spiritual training ground to expose the voices. His journal would be filled with insights about how he took his life back from them.

I wish you could have heard the fire in his voice. He was rearing to go!

The next thing I shared with him that I thought could help him was a principle I had learned from the monastery. This had to do with efficiency and time. At the monastery, I spent many years as the cook. It was the toughest job on the property. I can say that confidently because I had them all. But that's one of the reasons why I loved it so much. It was a big puzzle game of "how can I make this meal all come together and be amazing?"

Along the way, I mastered efficiency in the kitchen. While other cooks needed a team of people and hours to do the work, I often worked with only one other person. And we finished early with time to take a walk!

Everyone, including my teacher, was astonished by our accomplishments.

Because of my ability to be so effective, my teacher later changed up the rules for how the work periods would go for the other less efficient cooks. She saw what was going on. Instead of them getting several hours to complete a meal, they were given a single hour.

Wow, did that change up how good the cooks suddenly became! Now they needed to prioritize, strategize, and take the fewest possible steps to make meals happen. They could no longer sit around and become lost in conditioned mind. No lollygagging with the voices over the menu.

It was a truly brilliant tactic. And do you know what? The meals were produced perfectly. With the bonus of a transformed monk and spare time for other tasks to boot!

I shared this story with my client because I imagined he could apply this principle to his business.

Since he was an entrepreneur and he managed his own time, he had — in theory — 24 hours of his day dedicated to do his work. In his own words, his business was his "top priority," which was why everything else fell by the wayside.

Interesting how conditioned mind works: It's "all or nothing again!"

We were onto something here...

Now I gently asked him, "Is all of that time really being used effectively?" He admitted that it wasn't. He could relate to the monk who was lost in the voices over the menu. He saw how he was using the time he had and his attention poorly and therefore he was scrambling around putting out fires.

So as an experiment, we put a limit to the amount of time he would allot to his business. Just to see what happened.

Over the course of the next couple sessions, we talked about how his life restored itself to Pre-Crazy Time (PCT for short) with just a few simple shifts and the willingness to challenge the voices that screamed, "This won't work!"

We kept tweaking his approach and finding more-and-more time for what he loved and less time for ineffective, wandering unhappiness.

Oh, and his meditation time, walking time, and writing time increased. Just those small interventions of five minutes here, around the block there, and exposing how the voices worked in his writing created the foundation he needed for his motivation to explode.

How could he not be happy in his work when he felt so supported and cared for? His happiness spilled out from this foundation into his private life as well as his work life.

Because it was *all his life.*

Happiness is happiness. It's not in *what* you are doing. It's in *how* you are being.

And he chose his relationship with himself first, which in my experience always has the most profound effect on how you show up.

It creates the most powerful foundation for a beautiful life.

Results and control

A man prays at the altar, "O Lord, you know the mess I'm in, please let me win the lottery."

The next week, he's back again, and this time he's complaining, "O Lord, didn't you hear my prayer last week? I'll lose everything I hold dear unless I win the lottery."

The third week, he comes back, and this time he's desperate, "O Lord, this is the third time I've prayed to you to let me win the lottery! I ask and I plead and still you don't help me!"

Suddenly the clouds part and a booming voice sounds from heaven, "Benny, Benny, be reasonable. Meet me halfway. Buy a lottery ticket!"

My teacher shared this humorous parable with us in one of our group discussions at the monastery to illustrate that although life is *perfect* exactly as it is — ultimately, if we want certain results, we need to meet Life halfway.

This isn't about control. There is no control. Control is an illusion.

Yet Life asks us to meet it halfway if we want to co-create with it.

Yes, the body repairs itself perfectly. Yet it asks us to do what we can to take the best possible care of it: Eat nourishing foods. Exercise. Sleep well.

Yes, the mind's essential nature is clear, focused, and brilliant. Yet it asks us to do what we can to take the best care of it: Meditate. Stay present. Practice directing the attention.

Let's talk about results and control, because I get questions about these two topics frequently.

Results

Conditioned mind thinks in absolutes like, "If everything is perfect the way it is, why do anything?" So the answer is to do nothing.

Okay. We could go there. Or we could conclude that since everything is perfect the way it is, we can do *anything* we can possibly imagine. Instead of resignation, we can acknowledge that we have endless possibilities before us. We can keep going.

Every breakdown (something not going as I want) is an opportunity for a breakthrough (insight into possibility). I like to live in possibility because everything is my teacher if I allow it to be. I can choose to go full force with love and care, redirecting as needed in the moment and in the situation I am in.

I was the gardener at the monastery for several years. I would lovingly care for the seedlings the monks and I started in the greenhouse many months in advance of the planting season. I would water them, fertilize them, and give them access to sunshine and love. Then we would carefully transplant them into the garden, into soil that was perfect for them to thrive. We used black shade cloth for sensitive plants and white Reemay cloth for protection from insects. We employed a host of other preventative measures to ensure success since we decided to grow 100% organic. Our intention was to create a bountiful harvest.

We took tips from the best gardeners who were successful. We read books. We learned online and we grew from our own experiences and challenges.

Yet when those plants went down to some wandering gopher or suddenly die from an unexpected frost, it showed us our ultimate lack of control.

Control

Somehow it's the ego's entitlement that it gets exactly what it wants *when it wants it*. For some people, they can manage this for quite a while. I don't encourage it. I would suggest that for the lucky, this stops working as soon as possible.

Because attempting to control life is going to end someday. Who wants to go around in the delusional bubble of, "I'm immortal, my life is more significant than everyone else's, and life is about getting stuff for me and those I love," only to wake up abruptly to some accident, illness or death of a loved one and hope that the rebound will be with enlightenment instead of despair?

My wish for everyone is that we come to consciousness sooner rather than later. It's really the only intelligent choice. We're all headed into the ground with dirt shoveled over our faces or burned up to ashes. So we mustn't waste time avoiding practice.

I'm not saying this to depress anyone. I'm saying Life is meaningless. And we can choose the defeatist voice that says to us, "Why bother?" and just crawl under the covers. Or we can choose the *knowing* that screams, "Yeah, Life is *absolutely* meaningless! So I'm going to rise up unafraid to create something marvelous in the time I have here!"

It's time to stop waiting. Stop demanding "control" of everyone and everything around us. So we can see what's here before us as it is. Then ask, "What can be done with it? How can I love this moment fully? How can I *show up* in a way that furthers me toward results that are best for all? How can I take full responsibility for everything? How can I relinquish control so that something more amazing can reveal itself to me?"

To me, these are beautiful questions worthy of our time and respect.

Control asks no questions; It simply demands.

And this is why it fails.

Why are we afraid of getting what we want?

A: We're not. We're excited by endless possibilities. Our hearts leap for joy in the present moment. This *vitality* is our authentic essence.

However, the voices are terrified that we will keep our attention on those possibilities instead of with them. They distract us with their disappointments from the past and their uncertainties of the future. This is the bait they use to keep us engaged with them.

The fear we experience and believe is ours is really theirs. This is the fundamental truth we confuse and our opportunity for life changing freedom once we comprehend.

Test this out yourself. Find something you want that the voices scare you from having. Be sure that it is your heart's deepest desire. Next, make it a spiritual game to take steps toward it. That means take note of everything the voices say to you as you go about your day. Perhaps the first line you hear in your head is, "You're crazy! That's irresponsible!" Take dictation and confirm, "So, what I hear you saying is you think I'm crazy and it's irresponsible. Did I get that right? Is there more?" Then keep going.

In this spiritual practice, it's not so much the point to actually "get what you want" as it is to see how you *get stopped* on your way to getting what you want. When you understand how you are stopped in one way, you will likely see how you are stopped in all the other areas of your life. When you see through *how* resistance works, you can drop it and be free.

The voices aren't the voices of wisdom. They're not the voice of God. They have no real power over you. You are the one with the body. You are the one with endless possibilities abounding.

So when they talk, you just walk...

The gift

You can no longer just tell us what you believe in.

You cannot just sit back and be "for" or "against" anything. That's like saying you're opposed to children starving in the world and then doing nothing about it.

Opinions don't feed a single child.

You must not indulge the voices (internal or external) by remaining passive. Hearing the lie and then going along with it makes you an active participant who colludes with the lie.

Compassion, on the other hand, asks, "Given what's here — what now?"

It stands up and understands that the power of compassion lies in dropping the stories, getting present, taking a stand, seeing what's needed and then bravely taking action.

NOW.

The gift in having the voices of self-hatred in our lives is they require us to find compassion in every moment. For others and ourselves.

We cannot get complacent, go unconscious or assume the luxury of victimhood. The voices are our "worthy opponents" and we are up to the task of seeing beyond them. They would like for us to believe that they have all the power and that we can do nothing about them.

That is a lie. It is the illusion of their authority.

The gift shows up to demand that we wake up from our delusional slumber and actively participate in ending suffering.

The easy part is over. We saw it. We began meditating. We pushed a button. We cast a ballot. We said what we had to say.

Compassion then rolls up its sleeves and gets to work.

Herein lies the *real* gift: It never was up to them. It has always been up to *us*.

We must truly be the change we wish to see in the world.

God's dog

Robert Louis Stevenson encountered a man beating a dog. When Mr. Stevenson intervened on behalf of the creature, the man told him, "That's my dog and I'll treat him as I want." Mr. Stevenson replied, "No, that is God's dog and I am here to protect him."

My dog, my body, my kids, my refrigerator...

What else do we label and take ownership of that really isn't "ours?" How many other "things" do we mistreat or keep outside of compassion because they are not "ours" to care for? How many of "their" children or "their problems" do we ignore? How long must we mistreat ourselves? Why are we waiting for someone else to do something about it?

Why must we ration our love so much?

Another gift

'Tell me,' The Buddha asked a young man who was struggling with anger, 'if you buy a gift for someone, and that person does not take it, to whom does the gift belong?'

The young man answered, 'It would belong to me, because I bought the gift.'

The Buddha smiled and said, 'That is correct. And it is exactly the same with your anger. If you become angry with me and I do not get insulted, then the anger falls back on you. You are then the only one who becomes unhappy, not me. All you have done is hurt yourself.'"

I've shared this story about The Buddha in my coaching to illustrate that we have a lot more say in how we experience life than at first it may appear.

My clients tell me how stressed they are. They go on about how many emails they have in their inboxes to deal with and the endless obligations and duties expected of them. Their to-do lists of projects are daunting.

I interrupt them and have them breathe for a moment.

I ask them to consider if it's true that these external circumstances control their lives.

And they pause to consider the unfortunate truth.

You see, what they soon realize is that they assume every email is urgent and needs their immediate attention. They believe they must say "yes" to the endless requests being made of them and that immediate action is required for every project that passes across their desk.

All these urgent fires and endless desires seem to pull them away from *center*.

But what if being pulled away from center wasn't a requirement? What if they had a choice?

I'd ask them, "What if someone handed you a reason to be angry, or urgent, or distracted, or upset — and you *refused* to accept it? What would happen to it and the quality of your life?"

Please consider something you could practice with that you will use to master this skill.

Will you practice with your emails, your boss, your children or your anger?

How will you practice keeping your attention where you want it to be by not accepting "the gift?"

Love is not passive

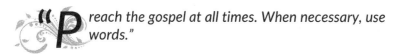 reach the gospel at all times. When necessary, use words."

~ St. Francis of Assisi

As long as we are listening to the voices in our heads, it is much easier to see the worst-case scenario rather than what is possible.

Which does not mean that I am advocating for wearing "rose-colored glasses."

There's a very popular assumption that "letting go" and "being in the present moment" looks like shrugging our shoulders and being passive. Resigned. Complacent. Agreeing.

I'm not suggesting that you turn your head away or live in a come-what-may frame of mind at all.

Instead, please consider the love of a mama bear as your role model. She defends, protects and cares for her cubs with outright ferociousness. She demonstrates love in action.

So the answer to life's challenges is not to give up. It is not a call to quit. You do not have the luxury to roll over and be quiet.

The voices of fear would rejoice if you complied. They have been attempting to squash you in every aspect of your life in which taking action mattered.

Instead recall the times you *did* take action. How did it feel to go up against the voices and see your challenge through to the other side? Weren't those moments of victory the cherished highlights of your life? The ones you remember with gratitude?

Focus on staying in action. Get up and take care of yourself: Meditate, stay fit, eat well, sleep, practice directing your attention to what you want it to be on, find something to be grateful for, help someone who is struggling, lift those who are down lower in spirits than you and form a plan to actively support what you value.

Please take a stand for *being* a force of love in the world.

Sorrow

 imes of great sorrow have the potential to be times of great transformation.

But in order for transformation to happen, we must go deep to the very roots of our pain.

And experience it as it is without blame or self-pity.

This pain is not to make you sad, remember.

That's where people go on missing....

This pain is just to make you more alert.

Because people become alert only when the arrow goes deep into their heart and wounds them.

Otherwise they don't become alert.

When life is easy, comfortable, convenient, who cares?

Who bothers to become alert?

Remember, the pain is not to make you miserable; the pain is to make you more aware!

And when you are aware, misery disappears."

~ Osho

If apathy and panic aren't the answer, what is?

Even when I was little I saw the craziness of duality in conditioned mind. I think I must have been born a philosopher who was always questioning and attempting to see through life rather than taking it at face value.

My training at the monastery helped me to see clearly the structure of how the voices worked to thwart human beings. Luckily for us, it always shows up in the same way. It's not very creative.

Either we swing to one side or the other to proclaim, *"The Answer."*

All or nothing. Good or bad. Black or white. Right or wrong. Love or hate. Us or them.

These are the structural posts of duality and the illusion of separation. And they are constructs of the mind.

It's what we habitually turn to when we describe what we are experiencing in life.

It is nearly impossible not to be forced to take one side or the other in the search for "where I stand."

I see it in the current two choices people habitually take: Either tuning everything out and going to complacency or acting out of panic, worry and obsession.

Both choices serve conditioned mind quite nicely and in some cases one is a reaction to the other. However, neither helps in any way whatsoever. They just siphon off the energy a human being could use to create something phenomenal.

What is that something phenomenal? The power love has given us to act.

When I trained at the monastery, one of the projects we created was helping a slum in Africa become self-sustainable. Not because there was something wrong that needed to be fixed, but because we could do it. We had friends who wanted to make this happen and we fell in love with the community. We saw it as a fun and worthwhile way to make a contribution to the world. And you know what? We benefited from the experience as well.

Best of all, we didn't have to make anyone wrong in the process. We didn't have to blame the African government. We didn't need to use guilt or shame to enroll people to join us.

Love guided us the entire way. And it attracted love from all around us.

When people are said to awaken, they describe the experience as their world becoming undone. Everything is revealed to be one and life is perfect as it is. There is wellbeing and the deep knowledge that there is nothing wrong. All is embraced in compassion.

I find the question, "What would love do?" to be a profound question to ask when confronted with uncertainty. And then to quiet the mind, remain in silence and wait for the answer. To not rush in with something. But rather allow the heart to reveal the answer.

We never know how the story will end

"Once there was a Chinese farmer who worked his poor farm together with his son and their horse. When the horse ran off one day, neighbors came to say, 'How unfortunate for you!'

The farmer replied, 'Maybe yes, maybe no.'

When the horse returned, followed by a herd of wild horses, the neighbors gathered around and exclaimed, 'What good luck for you!'

The farmer stayed calm and replied, 'Maybe yes, maybe no.'

While trying to tame one of wild horses, the farmer's son fell, and broke his leg. He had to rest up and couldn't help with the farm chores. 'How sad for you,' the neighbors cried.

'Maybe yes, maybe no,' said the farmer.

Shortly thereafter, a neighboring army threatened the farmer's village. All the young men in the village were drafted to fight the invaders. Many died. But the farmer's son had been left out of the fighting because of his broken leg. People said to the farmer, 'What a good thing your son couldn't fight!'

'Maybe yes, maybe no,' was all the farmer said."

A lot of love to Chance

At the monastery, I fell in love with a fluffy white and black cat that wandered onto the property. She was so beautiful. I remember that I took especially good care of her. I used to spend hours pulling the Velcro-like Burdock burrs that got stuck in her long fur when she came to visit my hermitage.

The monastery eventually decided that she was better off being cared for by someone else in the neighborhood. That meant I would never see her again. When I heard the news, I became quite sad. The day she was picked up by her new owners and gone for good was one of the hardest days in my training.

That night, I sat in meditation with tears streaming down my cheeks and asked a question, "How do you let go of someone you love?"

The answer that appeared was, "Love *everyone*."

I'll never forget the magnitude of that response. My heart opened beyond its broken capacity to include *all* of those around me so that it was impossible to experience loss.

This insight arose for me again today as my Colorado family and I took Chance, our 13-year old Golden Retriever, to the vet to be put down for his final rest.

It was a very hard week of seeing him extremely ill and especially hard to say goodbye to him this morning.

So I'm sending a lot of love to Chance, and in honor of him — to everyone too.

I love you.

I wish you well with it

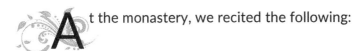**A**t the monastery, we recited the following:

"We are here to end suffering.

If ending suffering is more important than anything, we will end suffering.

If ending suffering is not more important than anything, we will not end suffering.

If I am suffering, it is because I am choosing something over ending suffering.

We are not here to create and cling to beliefs.

We are here to pay attention.

We are here to use everything in our experience to see how we cause ourselves to suffer so we can drop that and end suffering."

I remember several visitors and retreatants were offended by this recitation. In group discussions, they would incredulously ask, "What do you mean, 'I cause myself to suffer'? I don't want to suffer! The voices cause me to suffer — I get that — but I'm not choosing it. I'm a *victim* to it."

Well, I wish I could agree. But I cannot. When we are unconscious to the voices or are fooled by them and think they're us, yes, it's easy to see how we get stuck. It's like a character on stage playing their part *in* a drama. There is no other view. There is the life of that character. That character isn't the director or the audience having a disidentified view.

Anyone who has been doing this spiritual work, who has seen the "enemy", and chooses to believe the lies they spew *despite* knowing they're lies — well then something else is going on.

Almost nobody wants to grow up. We all want others to do what we want and we want to get what we want when we want it *all the time*.

This is the battle cry of egotistical children. They hold their breath until the adults give in. They believe their hero on a horse will ride in and rescue them from their pathetic lives.

We believe the seductive stories about how happiness is in the future and definitely *not* in this moment. We are looking to be saved some time *out there* in the distance so we can live happily ever after *then*.

The disappointing truth is that happiness is not an achievable goal. Once you possess what you think you want, it will dissolve into dissatisfaction and the next desire will show up in its place along with more dissatisfaction.

So the chase continues.

We need to take responsibility for dropping this chase. Drop it hard — like a hot potato. Just refuse to give an inch.

The voices are drug pushers that sell us dissatisfaction because we keep buying it. When we quit, we need to stay fixed on consciousness because those dealers are going to come around again. We bought before and they know we're good customers so you bet they'll come knockin' again.

Like Nancy Regan said, we need to keep saying "NO!"

People are not victims. They can *choose* to be, but I don't support it. I refuse to. I don't want to collude with anyone's desire to suffer. I don't want to enable people in their decision to be victims.

When I coach my clients, I take a hard line for them to be *free*. I tell them that I'm not fooled by who's who. I tell them, "You can play in your story but I'll have no part in it."

If I were working with you, I would team up with the part of you who loves you unconditionally and sees how freaking awesome you are — how working to free you can be *fun*! Now that's a mission worth giving a life to! That's someone I can take a stand with.

Because what's the alternative?

Well, that's just more of the same. And, "How's that going?"

I wish you well with it — until you're ready to let go of the struggle yourself. Whether you get worn down by it, fed up with it, or just plain give up, I do hope you eventually let go of it — sooner rather than later.

But until then, I wish you well with it.

How do I stop caring about what other people think of me?

 Stop caring about what *you* think of you.

Keep going

The degree of resistance the voices create to stop you is the degree of *vitality* waiting to fill you up on the other side of their resistance.

This is the counter-intuitive smokescreen the voices use to frighten you into believing you are somehow in danger. But the truth is that you are in danger with the thinking you have and the company you keep (with them).

If you feel depression, resistance, fear, worry, or doubt — a really good thing to know is that something amazing is waiting for you, *begging you*, to push through to the other side.

I've seen it over-and-over again. And whenever my clients share their resistance with me, I always enthusiastically encourage them to keep going. I yell at them, "That's great! This is a sign that you're on the right path! The voices are terrified that you'll be free of them!

Put the pedal to the metal and *go*! Do the opposite of what they say! Get to the other side!"

Your energy is yours. The voices talk you into feeling bad so they can convert that beautiful, vibrant energy into negative energy for themselves. But remember, you are the original source of all that energy. They can't consume it without your participation. It belongs to you, to use it as you please.

Therefore, keep your attention on what lights your heart up.

And keep going toward that light.

About the author

Alex Mill is a Zen Life Coach.

He trained in a Zen monastery for nearly 14 years. During that time he assumed various leadership roles in nearly every facet of the monastery's operation. From being the cook, to the gardener, to the work director, to the manager of the small business off the monastery's property, to the Sangha coordinator who made sure the practice stayed accessible to members far-and-wide.

He facilitated workshops and retreats as well as offered guidance appointments to Sangha members in-person and abroad.

Alex also created a cartoon series called *The Voices* that helped illustrate, in a humorous way, how all human beings are caused to suffer and how to end their suffering.

Today he coaches business professionals, out-of-the-box creative thinkers and entrepreneurs on how to overcome their biggest obstacles and create success from the inside-out.

Through private one-on-one coaching, a powerful online retreat, public talks and workshops, Alex shares what he learned in his Zen training to transform lives and businesses.

He continues to practice kindness and compassion for himself and others by loving life, practicing yoga, cooking whole food plant-based meals, learning, writing, painting and illustrating cartoons for his forthcoming book, *The Voices and What to Do About Them.*

You can learn more about Alex and his work by visiting his website at www.alexandermilljr.com.

Books by Alex Mill

Meditation and Reinventing Yourself
Practicing Presence

Online Programs by Alex Mill

Heart-to-Heart: Compassionate Self-Mentoring
Zen Meditation Circle
The Zen Life Podcast

www.alexandermilljr.com

A live, in-person extravaganza:

Reinventing Yourself Weekend

Join Steve Chandler, Karen Davis and Alex Mill for a crazy good time.

Reinventing Yourself Weekend will be full of fun, insight and transformation!

To read more and register, please visit:
www.reinventingyourselfweekend.com